T0191435

Rubies
in the
Mud

Rubies
in the
Mud

Terry Hauptman

Polaris
Publicattions

An impirint of
North Star Press of St. Cloud Inc.
www.northstarpress.com

Copyright© 2021 Terry Linda Hauptman

All rights reserved. No part of this publication may be reproduced, or transmitted in any form or by any means, electronic or mechanical, including photocopy, recording, or any information storage and retrieval system, without permission in writing from the author.

www.terryhauptman.com
terry.hauptman@yahoo.com

Published by Polaris Publications,
an imprint of North Star Press of St. Cloud, Inc.

Front and back cover paintings by Terry Hauptman,
as well as interior glyphs.
Cover Design by Liz Dwyer.

ISBN: 978-1-68201-116-4

First Edition

DEDICATION

For my sisters Joan Kahn and Helen Herman,
For my friends' communal cry,
My great grandparents and grandparents
visionary lives,
My mother Leonora's laugh
that dreams the wind,
For my father Jack's
generosity and care,
For Bob and Kira, rivering the land
For Atida Bernstein Ginsburg,
Reaching for the Stars.

For Liz Dwyer and Curtis Weinrich of North Star Press
for their visonary third eyes.

Gratitude for the mysteries

PRAISE

"Terry Hauptman envisions Quetzalcoatl 'laying her eggs in the Thunder's prayer,' and that is what Hautpman's poem-chants do. Mourning and celebration, fertility and terror twine together in these ecstatic performances. Hauptman honors her guardian spirits—Frida Kahlo, Lorca, Van Gogh, Chagall, Billie Holiday, Neruda; conjures the souls of her vivid ancestors, 'great grandpa Sam,' grandma Florence reading 'Dostoevsky at the back of a shoestore;' and grandmother Rae, the fortune-teller; mourns her mother, Leonora; and blesses her daughter and husband. Life and death embrace in the visionary wholeness of these poems."

-Rosanna Warren

"Underlying is her knowledge of spells..
Burns, seethes, gives birth in heat/
Heart...
To create a city of flames."

From *ON HEARING THUNDER*

-Joy Harjo
Poet Laureate

"Terry Hauptman's poetry is vibrant and full of life. These poems help us understand life in all its vitality. They lead us to a dynamic intersection where we experience many strands of human endeavor, beauty, spirit, frailty, myth, love, hope – some may be visible, some hidden, but all felt deeply by even a squinting eye. In "Angel with a Broken Wing 4" she writes about singer Paul Robeson and "his authentic vision illumined by fire". Terry always holds a torch for human equity. While doing so, her brilliant creative flame binds to oxygen and enlightens all of us with the rhythm, energy, mystery and wonder of *duende*. The hidden is revealed. Life is esteemed. This is poetry at its fullest, music, justice, bread, and ancestral bodies! Her ancestry is not clipped, instead it pivots into the future. It brings awareness and admiration while creating a new lineage. These works breathe beauty, creativity and insight from the heart of the vortex."

-Brian Fitzpatrick

"Poetry is another world
Poetry is thunder and lamentations
and sweet lingering joy
that we tap into—it reaches
for places in the heart and releases us
or makes us grieve more than we
expected to.
In the midst of all this is Terry's work.
Her poetry urges us to lament and to be joyful
such an undertaking and because her heart believes,
she is successful in this.

The poems are chronicles of our century and her imagination leads into the core events of a heartless time but there are the loving memories of her family which, strangely, saves all of us as we enter their lives.

The grandparents, aunts, uncles who lived eating joking finding safety in pickles, bread, and a loving recklessness—There is more the Mayans Spanish the history of the Americas—beauty, wisdom, rage, and hope.

This is both a poetry book and a history book and Terry presents all as one ongoing experience and we walk through it with her as our guide seeing what it is to be human."

-Barbara Clark

"In poet Terry Hauptman's latest book, Rubies in the Mud, her fortune-telling Grandmother Rae advises her to 'never tell the worst.' Hauptman admits that she is 'swallowing flies' but she also claims 'I never tell, the worst.' And so she doesn't on this journey. As readers Hauptman asks us to hear her calling and trust her vision; soon we are dancing to the center of the world joined by others: Thelonius Monk, Federico García Lorca, Louie Armstrong, the Angel of Longing, Cassandra on Asylum Street, the Boatman, Great Grandpa Sam, bees, prayers, Ava Maria, and the Dead Sea scrolls of Qumran. Hauptman's poems take us into the depth of night and speak the thunder of coming storms, inviting the *duende's* dark wisdom and power."

-Carmela Delia Lanza

"Malmoud Darwish said, 'Every beautiful poem is an act of resistance.' Terry Hauptman's new book, *Rubies in the Mud* exemplifies this. Like Denise Levertov, Hauptman does not shy away from the turbulence and tragedies of our time. She writes of the destruction of the Amazon jungle, the massacre at Parkland High School, the rising antisemitism, and bombings at temples, the fleeing refugees, the destruction of the seas.

She says 'James Baldwin writes on fire and wind' and so does Hauptman as she shows us beauty and splendor in nature and ordinary things. Her words reach towards the inner presence of light.

She speaks of the healing music of love: Billie Holiday whom she calls the 'Angel of Harlem' as well as Thelonius Monk, Louis Armstrong, and Josh White, who sing to the dead as well as the living. If the angels have broken wings, they continue to sing in the tents of Hauptman's praise.

She tells us that Paul Robeson was tragically stoned for his revolutionary heart but he is still a firebrand for change, and change is what we need in these troubled times. Terry knows her poems build on a legacy of work and gives credit to many of the writers she admires who have inspired her."

-Toni Ortner

Other poetry books by Terry Hauptman

Masquerading In Clover: Fantasy of The Leafy Fool
Boston: Four Zoas. 1980
(With hand-painted plates),

Rattle
Tulsa: Cardinal Press, 1982
(With an introduction by Meridel LeSueur)

On Hearing Thunder
St. Cloud, Minnesota: North Star Press of St. Cloud, Inc., 2004
(With color plates)

The Indwelling of Dissonance
St. Cloud, Minnesota: North Star Press of St. Cloud, Inc., 2016

The Tremulous Seasons
St. Cloud, Minnesota: North Star Press of St. Cloud, Inc., 2019

SHADOW GIFTS

All my life, I have tried to harmonize with others
In a round dance of fire
Circling around a breath
Of sacred prayer. . .
My mother humming.

ACKNOWLEDGMENTS

"Aleph," *Caliban Online* #38, 2020.

"Amulet," *Caliban Online* #40, 2020.

"Angel With a Broken Wing 3," *Caliban Online* #30, 2018.

"Angel With a Broken Wing 4," *Caliban Online* #35, 21, & 22;
   Contributor's Advice, 121, 122, 2019.

"Angel Of Harlem," *Caliban Online:* Contributor's Advice #34, 2019.

"At Empanadas Cafe," *Caliban Online* #37, 2019.

"Azure," *Caliban Online* #38, 2020.

"Beloved of the Soul 2," *Caliban Online*

"Blood Moon," *Caliban Online* #30, 2018

"Caracol Of Souls," *Vermont Views:* Monkey's Cloak, 2016,

"Caracol of Souls 2," *Caliban Online* #27, 2017

"Cupping," *Caliban Online* #40, 2020.

"Dark In Radiance," *Caliban Online* #37, 2019.

"Deep Song," *Caliban Online* #20; Contributor's Advice, 2020

"Deforestation," Caliban Online #38, 2020

"Dream," *Caliban Online* #30, 2018

"Duende's Black Sounds," *Caliban Online* #30, 2018.

"El Illuminado," *Caliban Online* #39, 2020.

"Extravagaria," *Caliban Online* #35, 2019.

"From The Book of Splendor," *Caliban Online* #27, 2017

"Heartbeat, For Leonora," *Caliban Online* #27, 2018

"Maestrapeace," *Caliban Online* #30, 2020.

"Mythographies/Diaspora," *Caliban Online* #27, 2017.

"Pandemic: The Fire In The Gods' Eyes," *Caliban Online*; *Contributor's Advice*, 2020.

"Parkland Students At The Center Of The World," *Caliban Online*.

"Return To La Paz: Peace Be With you," *Caliban Online* #30, 2018.

"Rubies In The Mud 2," *Caliban Online* #27, 2017.

"Struggle Is A Prayer For Hope," *Caliban Online* #31; *Contributor's Advice*, 2018

"The Caldera of Dreams," *Caliban Online* #39, 2018.

"The Psalms of Qumran," *Caliban Online* #40, 2020.

"Tribes: Desnos Reading The Palms of Men on Their Way To The Gas Chambers," *Caliban Online* #38, 2020.

"We Brake For Angels," *Vermont Views: Monkey's Cloak,* 2016.

THE FUTURE OF YOUR INSPIRATION

For Kira

You have been given the gift of love
From your soul house of compassion,
Walking in beauty's fire and light
   Let the winds breathe through you
   From your soul house of prayer
   That dreams the wind,
   Dreams the world
My Angel of The Americas,
You have been given the gift of love.
   Water lilies in a pond of frogs,
   Lilacs in the hemlocks and pines,
   Sparking the pulse of dawn,
   Listen to the sounds of life
   The azure of winds spiraling through you.

POEMS

AN INTRODUCTION

On a back road in West Wardsboro, Vermont, leading to the poet Terry Hauptman's home, there is a line of very old trees. We call them her guardian spirit trees for though, bent with time and gnarled, each returns to life each spring with crowns of green dancing leaves. They are a metaphor for her luminous poetry. Her soul roots are people's ancestral communal fires, their sacred texts and "songlines," all bursting into ecstatic dance, thrumming with the talking drums. Her poems hiss as well as roar against oppression, war, hunger, and pain. Rhythms of powerful essences, rhythms of resonance pulse into the medium of the word. Her gyratory dance gives power to the disinherited and the lost, the innocent victims of the world's bad karma. Terry whirls out her poems, burying rubies—the essences—in the mud of the deep forest's bear corridors as well as in the hot summer asphalt of city streets. Equipped with mystical knowledge, she spins out a hope that is found in the stars for the lost and the dead.

Growing up in New York, in neighboring Bronx and Queens, Terry's family's ancestral memories and history flowed around her. The city stirs her poetic soul when spending time with her sister, Helen at her home in Harlem. In new poems, she scries and creates a cadenced beauty and celebratory expression of street and urban life. The poem, "Breaking For Angels," written for Billie Holliday and Terry's sister, produces a world of musical praise for these angels of the heartbeat. Her cry of hope, here on city streets, whirls with *duende's* dark passion and reverberates in the "inviolet dark, under the ex-voto sky."

In Terry's poems dedicated to the loss of family members and friends, she honors the memories of the departed, the beloveds, in a deeply touching way. Ever present with their power of being, she moves them with spiritual tenderness through subtle metamorphoses to other dimensions. Reverberating with the teachings of Buddha and amplifying her mysticism, her studies of the Kabbalah and world shamanism—truths of the loved ones sing out in holy sparks and emanate love's flight to the spirit existing in all sentient realms. As she says in her poem "Aleph" dedicated to Jorge Luis Borges who wrote "Does the Aleph exist in the heart of a stone" Terry responds "Flinging destiny's winds into the open world of song, Fling fate into the heart's migrations, Fling emptiness into the resins of pine, "Does the Aleph exist in the heart of a stone?" Her response: "That azure sap of mountain thunder humming within."

As she pauses in her lyric dance, she gathers the profound essences and vitality of life into her poetry. She listens for that humming muse of call and response: "finding the rubies in the mud," "salt music from the honeycomb hive."

-Jeanne Joudry, artist

Stratton, Vermont

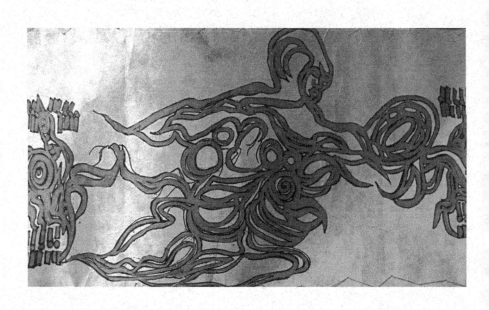

RUBIES IN THE MUD

"Eye of the heart"

-Rumi

"Todas las casas
hacia su presencia
Everything is fleeing
Toward its presence"

-Roberto Juarez

"Every beautiful poem is
an act of resistance"

-Mahmoud Darwish

"So beautiful, it burns"

-Kira Hauptman

RUBIES IN THE MUD

The angel's gold leaf
  Luminous in the catacombs of wasps
    Blesses the swarming psalms
     Shattered in the baths of lust.

Palms of fate
  Predict fortunes that bind,
    As desire undulates
     In the mineral divine
      Eating the heels of rye bread and soot
      With my Great Grandma Rae
       On the Coney Island boardwalk,
      "Never tell the worst,"

Burying rubies in the mud
  Eye-of the heart
    Lost in the music of love.

RUBIES IN THE MUD 2

From The Hummingbird Sanctuary Of Kukulkán

Quetzalcoatl throws off black sparks
Laying her eggs in the thunder's prayer
Holding our babies under the ceiba trees
Beside the strumming of guitars.

I warm myself
By the dark-hearted bees
That spark the hive.
Wash my hair with lavender and mint
Near Huitzolpochitli's eye of god,
And Popocatépeti's volcanic peaks,
As crows in the wolves dollhouse
Knead angel bread,
Salt the black earth

    Oh Sister,
    Dancing at Bayamos
    Wearing your red dress
    Playing your flute at
    Sweet Water's and Small's Paradise
    Dance with me
    As old trees
    Spin the wheel of K'mesh,
    Exiled in birch and mountain ash
    Where hornets nest
    Throwing rubies in the mud,
    The indwelling of light
    Piercing the moon,
    As the winds return
    Calling me.

ANGEL OF HARLEM

For Billie Holiday
And for my sister, Helen

Hummingbirds at the Arab grocery store
    On Broadway
        Dive for gardenias
            As Billie Holiday sings
                "Strange fruit from Southern trees"
            On the airwaves outside,
"Strange fruit,"
    The song immortalized by Billie Holiday,
        Written by Abel Meerpole,
            Aka Lewis Allen,
                Our father's social studies teacher
                    At De Witt Clinton High School
                      In Washington Heights.
Oh sister
    Walking with you on Harlem streets
        Dreaming the blues
            Trembling in the zig-zag pulse
                Of Grandma Rae's
                Fortunetelling winds
Singing to the dead
    And the living
        Through the Kabbalah flamed incantations,
            Remembering when you rose up
                At Sweetwater's and Small's Paradise,
            Fluting the bones,
                Eating black beans and rice,
            At Flor de Mayo
                And Floriditas,
With Billie Holiday
    The Angel of Harlem
        At the center of the world.

ANGEL WITH A BROKEN WING 3

Draw your bow into the wolf's smoke,
  The bear's breath
    On the corridor of hope
      Deer dance dervish
        Thrumming with doves
          Where peacocks sound like hinges
            As saxophones cry
              Sounding "Sweet Honey In The Rock."
Your clattering piano-key teeth
  Sing the blues
    Ululating like coyotes
      Walking down freedom road
        "Ain't gonna let nobody turn me around"
Shekinah in the tents of praise
  Fermenting the willow-sap
    Resins of Baal
      In the forest's
        Home for the blind. . .
          Angel with a broken wing.

ANGEL WITH A BROKEN WING 4

Piercing the deep pines' moonlit sky
  Licking honeysuckle at Jacques Dubois'
    Listening to old Aunt's talk of free love on porches
      Eating bowls of scallions and sour cream
        Licking pollen in the dream world of fate
          Following crows to Mohegan Lake
            Near Peekskill New York,
              Where Paul Robeson was vilely stoned
                For his revolutionary heart,
My aunts and uncles wept for days and nights
  For his brilliant voice,
    His authentic vision illumined by fire,
      Bringing down the light
        For civil rights,
          The soul's bread
            In the palm of his hand,
              A firebrand for change and love.

STRUGGLE IS A PRAYER FOR HOPE

For Devin Balcacer

> *"Mi corazón como una sierpe,*
> *se ha despiendido de su piel,*
> *y aquí a miro entre mis dedou,*
> *llena de heridas y de mie!*
> *Like a snake, my heart*
> *has shed its skin,*
> *I hold it there in my hand,*
> *full of honey and wounds."*
>
> *-Federico García Lorca*

We walk to the Magic Theatre
  On 125th Street in Harlem,
    Passed the Soul Saving Center
      Across the street
        Where love and death
          Transform each other
            In the music of winds
              Listening to Ernesto de la Cruz sing
                "Remember Me."
                  As the wolf moon
                    The cold moon
                      Cries the blues.
The raven ruins luminous with hope
  Tremble beneath our feet
    As roundups in sanctuary cities
      Rip us apart
        Listening to the dead sing
          The honey of longing.
            Dreamers on La Salle
              Yearn to breathe free
                Bearing witness to healing prayers
                  In the ex-voto dolor of night.

The dreams of strangers
  Leading us home
    Passed owls at hospice
      Hooting snap-chat instagram ghazals,
        Passed the holy relics
          In Dominican hotels,
            Lorca's New York streets coming alive
            Licking scarlet from destiny's hive.

AT EMPANADA'S CAFE

For my sister, Joan

> *"Oh I love moonlight*
> *And I love starlight,*
> *And I lay this body down."*
>
> *-Josh White*

My mother Leonora humming at Empanada's Cafe
 In Louis Armstrong's old neighborhood
  On 108th Street
   In Corona Queens,
    Listening to his blue notes riffs
     "Nobody knows the trouble I've seen,"
      Tree of Life Trumpet
       Remembering Satchmo's house
        On 107th Street
         Near the Lemon Ice King
          Of Corona.
I wanted Blue Monk's sound
 "Round Midnight" "Strait No Chaser"
  To pierce my painted scrolls.
   Miraculous music syncopating
    Armstrong's heartbeat
     "When the Saints Go Marching In"
Spirit Moves Life
 Life moves Spirit
  Climbing the seven steps to heaven
   Improvising jazz dissonance
    From your trumpet
     Above and beyond.

TRIBES

*"Desnos Reading The Palms of Men
On Their Way To The Gas Chambers"* *
-Stephen Berg

In The Book of Why
History torques
The thunder's burnt tears
In the city of dreams.
Your garnet eyes remember
"Desnos Reading The Palms of Men
On Their Way to the Gas Chambers"
In Buchenwald
Predicting Good Fortune
Before they perish forever.
This day of At—One—Ment
In the winds of lamentation
In the pomegranate ash
Maror and tar,
I wonder about Desnos' optimistic gift.
Wearing malachite, the thorned jewel
Of my tribe's dust,
Drinking Sangría
In El Farro's Spanish Restaurant
Where James Baldwin
Used to laugh
Writing on Fire,
Writing on Wind,
In the burnished sun
Burnt-earth silhouette
Of Freedom.

* "It is reported that the French poet Robert Desnos broke out of line of naked prisoners on their way to the gas chambers at Buchenwald and went from prisoner to prisoner reading their palms, predicting good fortune and happiness. My friend, Bill Kubrik, who has translated Desnos' poetry in his book, *The Voice*, told me this story."

-Steven Berg

*Robert Desnos died in Terezinstadt two days after the camp was liberated by Russian troops.

DUENDE'S BLACK SOUNDS

For Thelonious Monk   (1917-1982)

Duende's black sounds
  Dolor of forgotten dissonance
    Master of what's beneath the melody
      Heart and soul of
        Betty Carter's dream flame
       Piercing your Fado soul
Blue memory of black Madonna's at the piano
  Your keyboard sounding hyacinth riffs
    Salt music from the honeycomb hive
      Trembling on Furnace Street
       At the Old Paris Flea Market, Alive,
        Thelonious, we are calling you,
        Calling you.

THE CALDERA OF DREAMS

Love, love a flock of deer,
    Hare's breath of hyacinth fire
        Snow owl
            Witnessing the votive dawn.
I recognized the fox
    By the zig-zag part in her silver hair,
        The fawn by the mystery in her gaze,
        The wolf by her nurturing heart,
            Spirit of the wind calling me.
I cut the earth to find my poems
    Turning life inside out,
        On the caldera of dreams
            Following the forest mystics'
            Shema of sacred deer
                Down to the river
Following their music
    Through the lightning and winds,
        Calling to the disappeared
As The Malack Ha Moves
    The Angel of Death
        Moves over us.

THE PSALMS OF QUMRAN

I dreamed of the Bedouin Shepherd
Looking for his lost goat
And finding
Scrolls in ceramic pots,
The night after viewing
The Blood and honey
Dead Sea Scrolls of Qumran
At Jerusalem's Shrine of The Book
With wonder.
Memory scrolling blessings
In tablets lost in storms
In the dybbuk clay of Aramaic joy
Fanned by date-palms
From the psalms of Baal,
The honeyed ash of lost souls.

AMULET

The green humming
  Of telluric sparks
    Honeyed by sulfur
      Wakes the dead
        Through a spiral of gall.
Your black eyelids charred by ash
  Blink at crows
    Dancing at the center of the world.
Blue sap of the ambers
  Shimmers in the deep.
    Who, in The Book of Splendor
      Rises from the dead
        Walking backwards
          In the dreamworld of fireflies
Cantillating into the dark
  On Furnace Street,
    Drawing us down
      Into the great mysteries?

WE BRAKE FOR ANGELS

I dream as I lay at the edge of the city of love,
Dancing flamenco on La Salle
And at the Apollo Theater in Harlem
Where the homeless, let out from Riker's Island
Swoop down for eternal bread

Graffiti scrawled out...
sic... transit.

We brake for angels
As the spirit passes through
Trembling in summer heat
On Dr. Martin Luther King Drive,
Taking selfies
In the city of dreams,
Scattering the deep mineral particles of soul.

Listening to deep music
On Riverside Drive
That marks freedom.

Each kiss foreshadowing fear,
Besieged as new mothers cry
Their green willow prayers
Wearing destiny's necklace of stone tears
As the sky turns red

Dreaming the divine presence
Of Martin Luther King and

Abraham Joshua Heschel
Walking the Freedom March

From Selma to Montgomery
Standing strong
In the firelight of song.

ALEPH

"Who if I cried would hear me among the angelic orders?"

-Rainer Maria Rilke

"Does the Aleph exist in the heart of a stone?"

-Jorge Luis Borges

Tell me how the Angel of Longing flies through your soul.
Who, in the Book of Splendor dreams the open dark?
Listening to ululating coyotes
Flinging destiny's winds
Into the open world of song,
Fling fate into the heart's migrations,
Fling emptiness into the resins of pine.
"Does the Aleph exist in the heart of a stone?"
That azure sap of mountain thunder
Humming within.

BELOVED OF THE SOUL

*"A mosaic is a conversation between
what was broken."*

-Terry Tempest Williams

BELOVED OF THE SOUL 2

"Each of us can receive
the mystery of the other."
-René Char

Beloved Of The Soul,
Draw your heart-bow,
Cast your fate in sulfurous winds,
Fleet-footed as a deer,
I run towards you

    Pine-pitch of the raven's caw
    The green trees wrap around us,
    As night falls away.

Beloved of the soul,
Draw your heart-bow
Through the hemlock soot of night,
Ululating coyotes hear your song,
The joy of love
Through the pines.

Wandering through the Vía Dolorosa
    Sending light down through Malkuth's crown
      Passing the blue salt of Teppirah
        In the rapture of song
          The comings and goings of angels
          In tablets lost in storms.

CARACOL OF SOULS

How light travels through the body's
  Blue mists and rains,
    Zigzags like music
      Through your song of flames.

Listening to Yasmin Levy's "Me voy"
  "I'm leaving,"
    Watching locusts eating angel bread
    In the ancient darkness
      Of Ein Gedi
        On El Día de Los Muertos
        The Day of The Dead

Wearing Frida Kahlo's hummingbird-thorn necklace
  Black Madonna of the insect's thorax,
  Forgetting the tabernacle of the heart's kiss
    Listening to Romanian gypsy riffs,
    The Archeology of he Soul,
      As love dies in its fulfillment
        Despite it's promise.

CARACOL OF SOULS 2

"Don't go listening to those starry-eyed Cassandra's
   On Asylum Street
      Singing from the dark."
         Watching the wind's green dress
            In the tides of fate
               As children sip
                  The willow sap of Ur,
                     While old women
                        Pour libations
                           For the days
                              To come.

HEARTBEAT:

From The Book Of Splendor: Rosh Hashanah

Aleph, Mem, Shin,

Ox, Water, Tooth

Pamela White Hadas

When Great-Grandma Tamara left her
    Minsk-Gibernia shtetl,
        Carrying silver candlesticks
            To New York's Lower East Side,

Chagall's green violin followed her
    Fleeing   pogroms
        Burying her dead son at sea,
          My grandma Lillie
            And her sister Sarah
             Looking on

Never to return
    As blackbirds nest in Malkuth's crown,
      Hamseh, the third eye in her palm,
        Ruach's spirit breath
         In The Book of Life,
            Soul that breathes the mystery's
            Blue thunder
              Through the generations.

MYTHOGRAPHIES

Diaspora

The day my great grandpa Sam's coffin
Fell from his third story apartment,
His pine box opened up
And his body fell down the stairs
Passed the porch glider and seltzer bottles,
Into the mists and rains.

He was a carpenter who lost his finger
    In a chopped liver grinder
While building pine coffins during the war.
Dreaming of herring and black bread
    Served at the Shiva

The one eyed crow
Listening to the Moma-Loshen Mother Tongue
    Yiddishkeit of Workmen's Circle Jews
        From Belarus
            Ibn Gubenor Ben Jews,
                Secularists of the Bund
                Returning
                    To dance in the New Year
                    With Bertha Kalish,
                    The Sappho of the
                        Yiddish Theatre
                    Walking through his soul.
                    It is fated.

AS WE COME MARCHING, MARCHING:

Legacy

For Grandma Florence

Leaflets fall from your ribcage.
You read Dostoevsky at the back of a shoe store,
You read The Daily Worker at the window of a cafeteria,
You tell me Aunt Becky was blind from rubbing dust rags
  Into her eyes,
Charlie, with his pajamas under his work clothes,
Will change the world.
Trotskyite woman, Wobblie wife,
You want Bread and Roses too,
You paint a lifeline   set it on fire,
Pinch me when you name me
"My Life" "My Life."

My Grandparents, Florence and Charlie Herman, in Chelsea, New York, marching against Hitler. Circa 1940.

RETELLING

Tell me about the journey, Grandma
The one from Minsk to New York,
Your brother flung to fishes, overboard,
Thrust back to Russia with smallpox fever.
Then steerage again,
Strong immigrant child,
Your father build boxes of pine,
Your husband's eyes were given to science,
Your baby died,
Your spirit surviving and blazing with kindness,
Oh tell me about the journey, Grandma
That I may sweetly kiss your beet-stained hand.

CUPPING

My grandma Lillie
  Lined up her small blue
    Vicks Vapor Rub bottles
      On her sister Sara's back,
        Struck a match
          To draw out the poisons
            From within

Smoking the medicine
  Into her skin. . .
    Heat like wasps'
      Burning winds
        Redolent of music.

Grandma singing,
  "Come on a my house,
    My house a come on"
"I'm going coco-loco
  In my cocoa,"
    Before visiting Grandpa
      At Mt. Hebron Cemetery
        In Queens,

Wearing her red dress
  From the camphor cedar chest,
    Singing in a minor key
      For life, for love,
        Improvising in the lilac dawn
          As the winds broke open.

POST CARD

For fortuneteller Great Grandma Rae

I am giving a reading,
Reading the bones,
The ones you read at Coney Island
Before the termites took over. . .
The piano fell through the trap door.
I want you to know, I too am an 'a card'
Vaudevillian poet, all dead-pan alley
Like a blind-seer, crafty with life,
Alive with slapstick,
I'm swallowing flies,
Like you,   I never tell,   the worst.

YOU FOLLOW THE STARS

For Grandpa Charlie

"Lo que quedaba después que el viejo amoroso el viejo
dulce, habla pasado ya a ser la luz
y despaciosísimamente era arrastrado en los rayos postreros
    del sol,
como tantas invisibles cosás del mundo."

"All that was left after the loving man, the kind old man
had passed over into light
and was slowly, slowly pulled off in the last rays
  of the sun,
like so many other things we cannot see in this world."

               -Vicente Aleixandre, Translator: Lewis Hyde*

Oh Grandpa you magician, how's tricks?
Remember the hat: 2¾**
Rhinestones in shoe boxes,
Your wild dance at Bickford's?
Rolling lemons up your sleeves,

How we would dance for you, dance for your socialist
    dreams,
Your songs aired and trumped in the light,
The leap through flames where Charlie shouts
  "I'm cooked."

Gingersnapping zu-zu to pluck up a semmel
Your feet in a bucket, from gout,
How you would whirl to lose direction
Blinded in snow
Return to dance on your tar roof,
Pluck up a syat,
The purple veins twisting in your nose,

33

Your heart,
Your final wink,
Then silence.
You are gone.

*From Aleixandre's poem, "The Old Man and the Sun."

**2¾ was the password for conscientious objectors, like my grandfather, crossing into Canada from the United States, refusing to serve during the first World War. 2¾ was a very small hat size, a call and response "remember the hat," and the response would be: "2¾."

SLIVER OF MOON FROM THE OPEN WINDOW

For Great Grandma Tamara

This September night
As you dip your stale bread in pickle juice   singing
"*Danke Gotte, Liebe Gotte,*" for this and for everything,
As you turn the mattress looking for bedbugs,
Wabble in galoshes, eating *sjav* and *kasha,*
Yiddish babushka   Hag of the backstore rubble,
Walking the Brooklyn Streets,
Pike and carp swimming in your bathtub
Waiting to become gefilte fish.
"*Go vey* from donnin"
You cry out, as you had cried out
"*Bumaka,Bumaka*"
When Grandma bobbed her hair,
Or when Grandpa Sam
Lost his fingers in the chopped liver grinder.
My mother is afraid of you,
Zeis Keit Gottinieu,
Calls me a witch
And names me after you,
Sweetheart.

HEARTBEAT 2

For my mother, Leonora

On National Black Theatre Blvd
  Off 125th Street
    Passed Malcolm X Blvd in New York City
      Listening to the sulfurs of blue-toothed jazz
        Lady Day swooning the streets
          While crowds outside the Apollo theatre on 125th Street
          Memorialize Prince's "Purple Rain"
            Your black butterfly soul appears to me
              As subway dissonance pulses
                The sistole/diastole of the heart.

Coming home from the hospital,
  I think about my ninety-one year old mother's
    Loss of memory
      Salt-glaze on Lost Road,
        Her long memory still holding ancestral tales
          Delighting us all
            As black eyelids close
              Over the third-eye of story.
              My mother dreams of crossing over
                The blue waters to see everybody
                  Blessing them as her spirit rises up
                  Into the Raven ruins
                    Singing the Hudson River's caw.

YAHRZEIT

For my mother Leonora   (1925-2018)

> *"Dance me to your beauty*
> *with a burning violin.*
> *And dance me to the*
> *End of Love"*
>
> *-Leonard Cohen*

September's blue flames
  Shadow the world with longing
    We dream
      On the bear corridor
        Under the sweet gum,
        Liquid amber moon.
Loss envelopes us
  Listening to nightbirds call
    to Leonora
      Buried in Queens.
        The bard owl on the playhouse
          Hisses a cry of grief
            Black resins fill the sky
              With the soul's soot
                From backyard blown glass
We sip mint tea
  On grandma's cross-stitched tablecloth
    Stained by sumac
      And blue—eyed grass.
            That was when yearning went right through me.
              That was when the red thread of fate
                Wrapped around me.
Dancing with a burning violin
  Into the river's dark
    Licking honey from
      The stain of deep love
        Licking honey from
          Rubies in the mud.

WORLDS BELOW AND ABOVE

For Leonora

My mother is on a boat
  Headed for the horizon. . .
    Oh the boat is returning
      In the half-light of dreams.

My mother is headed out to sea
  Headed for the underworld
    Past the boatman
      Who ferries the dead
        Over the River Styx.

My mother is peaceful
  And smiles as she floats
    With her eyes closed
      Humming
        Into the next world.

YOUR FINAL ALCHEMY OF SOUND

For my mother Leonora (1925-2018)

You passed into the winds of change
   Like a song

Leonora, you closed your eyes
   And died into the morning
     Wanting to end your pain

Shimmering in the sleek light
   Of the kabbalist's divine,
     The look of fire in deathwinds
       Before your final ascent
         To the stars.

Your violet flame
   Longing for the infinite silence,
     The last blue salt of the olive,
       Black bread and salt cakes for the dead,
     Moaning for the soul's transcendence.

Crying in rain
   You passed into the winds of change,
     Your death cry making your way
       Through the ancestral dark,
     Telling us you loved us,
         Your final alchemy of sound.

SONG FOR MY FATHER

For my Father, Jack Herman (1923-2006)

Named after John Reed

And Eugene Victor Debs

"This little light of mine

I'm going to let it shine"

You cry out from your hospital bed
  In the mineral dark
    As death dreams the wind,
      The singing wind,
        Sing sorrow,
          Singing sorrow
Remembering Horace Silver's
  Song For My Father,
    Strumming folk songs on your guitar,
      Loving your children, so desperately,
        Laughing in the fields where the wild lilies grow,
          Painting blue spruce in hurricanes,
            As the winds of promise
              Fade into the night,
                Burnt lilacs in the lightning's wing,
        Sing sorrow,
          Singing sorrow,
As you sing with my mother
  Like Les Paul and Mary Ford
  "Vaya con Dîos my darling,
    May G-d be with you, my love."
Harmonizing at midnight
  In the flames of love,
    Laughing with blackbirds
      In the house of song.
        Then the sky broke open,
          As if to speak:
            Rest In Peace

MAYDAY

For my sister, Joan

In sounding rain, we syncopate the spring rite.
Jonah with your tambourine
Into each ray spirals.
La Gioconda, Isadora, Gemini,
You are Leonardo's woman
Smiling in mystery's pulse and breath,
Teaching children from all tribes
Dancing the rhythms of memory
Writing the alchemy of Souls,
I honor the beauty that resides
Within you,
Radiant and bold.

TALKING WITH G-D

For Kira

Talking with G-d in the Sephardic winds of music,
The ancient Jewish blues of the piyyot,
Longing for you
In the Chilam Balam of Chumayal
With the Jaguar priests of the Yucatán.

    Praying for you
        With my palabras del corazón
    At the Santuario de Chimayó
    With El Cristo Negro,
    The Black Christ of Esquípulas Santo Niño
        Concealed in the green winds of Guatemala's clay.

Eating the tierra bendita,
The blessed earth,
Opening the door to the spirit world,
I look to the ceiba tree, the wisdom tree,
Listening to the black earth in her mystery,
The Tree of Life in the palm of my hand.

RIVER OF STONE

Wrapping you in the dybbuk clay of migrations,
In the half light of flowering stone,
Crying to the highest power of Guatemalan mothers
Under flowering volcanoes
In cordillera horse dreams
As our souls meet the dawn,

    Driving through a Minnesota blizzard
        Through the passions of a century
    To bring you home to us,
    To bring you home.

BLUE HERONS ON THE MISSISSQUOI RIVER

Vermont

For Roxanne Bogart

Blue herons on the Mississquoi River
  Rise up singing
    Over the dark waters,
      High up in the trees
        Where the cormorants scud

Throw their fledglings to winds
  On the river's pulse
    Listening to the blue waters
      Of forever
        Spark the promise of song

Laughing with children
  Wearing life-vests
    In our boats

      Watching our daughters
        In love with life
          Bathe in the
            Music of love
              Tremulous
                As warblers throats.

RESONANCE OF RAIN

For Bob

Loving each other in the pines and sugar maples
  Walking with you
    Through the blue mud
      To our forest home
        On the bear corridor
          Of blood-root and ash
        Lilacs and nettles
        The blue sky
          Rivering beauty
Where we walked
  Throwing salt over our shoulders
  Climbing our ladder
    Through dreams'
      White pines and mountain ash
      Saying yes
        To our union
          Under the stars
          The night leaves
           Falling, falling.

West Wardsboro
Vermont

FLAMES FERMENTING

"Before you know what kindness really is
You must lose things."
-Naomi Shihab Nye
For Derora Bernstein (1942-1977)

Hands in the grave-diggers' bees
Wedding dress turned to dust
Firefly moon extinguished
"Wedding canceled due to illness."

RIVER OF DAWN

For Derora Bernstein   (1942-1977)

River of dawn shivering death shriek,
  Derora,
Cold waves swallowing salt,
  The spirit breath dark on the horizon,
Dark winds, crawling misstep,
  Black dawn,

Oh, sister, Shekinah,
  Ring of fire,
    River drone,
      Rose kiss of the morning
       Falling, falling,
Dark winds, blood anemone.

What wisdom, the river,
  The golem bellied tree?
Deep in your rivered
  Dybbuk womb,
    The horned lizard
      Climbing blood-winds
      Root by root

Scree of earth
  Crying death shriek
    Ring of fire
      Rose kiss of the morning,
       Falling, falling.

DANCE TO THE END OF LOVE*

"We know something that is real,
The hearts of our friends."
                    -Eduardo Galeano

For Atida Bernstein Ginsburg (1950-2018)

The leaves heart-shaped, red bud
   Blur the mists and rains
      Salt glaze of sacred sparks
      Scats the tree of life

Lost friends dance
   Guided by voices
      As the night falls back
      Singing

*Song by Leonard Cohen

48

DREAM

Selfie's mark your generation
   A GPS of the Soul's
      Shape-shifting music
         Stops for death on a pale horse
        At the wolf's doll house.

Pentecostal memory guides your spirit
   As the wind breaks free in the mysteries.

     Ghost peppers stop your breath
      Annihilating your hunger
       Bartering for snails
         Drenched in sweet decay
           Shimmering with destiny
         In the hip-hop dark.

Tell me why your body (a temple)
   Disintegrates to ash
     As the sky turns red.

     I scream
      "Hold me close and hold me tight"
        From the wolf tremolo of inferno dreams

       "Rise up from the mercy of night
        And walk in beauty."

DARK IN RADIANCE

*"And I tell you that you should open yourselves
to hearing authentic poets of the kind whose
bodily sense were shaped in a world
that is not our own and that few people are able
to perceive. A poet is closer to death than
philosophy, closer to pain than
intelligence, closer to the blood."*

-Federico García Lorca

BLOOD MOON

For Federico García Lorca (1898-1936)

> *"It is the intimate sap*
> *that ripens the fields,*
> *the blood of the poets*
> *who loosened their souls*
> *to wander all the ways*
> *of nature"*
>
> > *-Lorca*

Chimeras of bliss and false promises
Shatter starry nights
Cerulean with love.
Chimeras of grief and false promises
Shatter starry nights
In the blue flames of loss.

You slow dance through the ghost memory
Of gypsy jazz
Honeying the lilac dark
Under the full sap moon.
How your waters rise up discordant
In ecstasy
As red-throated hummingbirds arc over you
Emptying yourself into your lover's arms
Painted with gesso and gall,
Embracing your secret fires, azul.
Before you are murdered
By the fascists
Shot down in Granada
With dead bees
Murdered under the gypsy moon's
Duende of dying stars

REVELATIONS

For Vincent Van Gogh (1853-1890)

"Well, my own work, I am
risking my life for it and my reason has half foundered."
Letters from Vincent to Theo,
July 1890

"Painting is inborn,
Theo, but not as most suppose. No,
You must put your hand out, reach for it,
grasp it -- painfully obvious. I know,
only by painting one becomes a painter.
I, Vincent, Poems from the Pictures
of Van Gogh"
-Robert Fagles

Blood burns your starry night soul,
  Hidden like vermilion crows
    Over the wheat field.
Old peasants
  In the raven ruins of forgetting
    Bend down in salvation
      Dreaming ploughed fields
As anguished brush strokes
  Spiral flaming cypresses,
    Haunting spires,
      In the minor keys
        Of strength and hope.

Painting your blood-red and billiard green
  Night cafe,
    Your soul luminous with grief,
      Trembles in the mysteries'
        Dispossessed promise
          Of life and death.

Your earth bound
   Salt of the earth sacrament
      Of violet rain
         Sparks cobalt and cadmium clouds,
            At the Asylum of St. Rémy.

So unlike the others,
   Crying into your
      Secret life of praise,
         No one noticing the ecstasy
            You felt in the landscapes' breeze,
               World open to the smoke of bees,
                  Starry palette of heartbreaking belief,
                     Painting your evanescent carmine
                        Of the gaslight's song,
                           "Our brush strokes burning clearer
                              Into dawn." *

Painting pure color,
   Leaf-green and iris
      Chromatics,
         The blood and ash azure of vineyards,
            Branching the olive groves'
               Gospel of teal,
                  "The best revenge is painting well."*

* From *I, Vincent, Poems from the Pictures of Van Gogh*,
   by Robert Fagles.

OROZCO'S SORROWS

"Holding the worms between my fingers in prayer."*
-Carmela Delia Lanza

When I met the Black Madonna
　　Drinking Añil de Muerto
　　　　On Calle Lorca
　　　　　　On El Dîa de los Muertos
　　　　　　The day of the Dead,
Voices from the graves rose up
　　From their Moorish sleep
　　　　In the arroyos of sheep
Dancing boleros,
　　Listening to the pungent surging
　　　　Of bees
　　　　　　Ruffling the wings of intimacy
Who listens in the raven ruins
　　Painting Orozco's sorrows
　　　　With resins of blood
　　　　　　Piercing our dreams?

*From her poem "Grace" in *So Rough A Messenger.*

RUACH

For Marc Chagall   (1887-1965)

Ruach's blue flames dance
  Over the rooftops of praise
    Like Chagall's lovers'
      Deep moan over the waters,
        Of desire
          Rising into beauty
            With prayer shawls
              Floating in winds'
                Eternal pleasures
                  Radiant with love.
Blue resins of the Zohar's breath
  Syncopating song,
    Beloved of the soul,
      Praying
        In the painted pulse
          Of green violins'
            Pungent surging entwined
            In lapis skies
Looking out from the shtetl smoke of Vitebsk's
"I and My Village"
    Floating with ladders
    Over the world
Your paintings
  Restoring intimacy
    To its ancestral place
    Under the stars.
Dancing with a burning violin
  Into the mineral world
    Licking honey from
      The stain of deep love
        Licking honey from
          Rubies In the Mud.

WAITING FOR WINDS

For Garrett and Keo

Reading poetry at Theatre 80 at St. Mark's Place,
　　Dreaming about Lord of The Sky Mountain in Laos,
　　　　Whose tip is always in the clouds
Waiting for the winds
　　To celebrate the ruins
　　　　Of The Dawn of Happiness,
　　　　　　Where civets rule
　　　　　　　　The winds' migrations
Temples reach for the lightening's mandala of sound,
　　Garret and Keo singing at spiritual reservoirs
　　　　And reflecting ponds,
　　　　　　As the kingdom of a million rice fields,
　　　　　　　　The kingdom of a million elephants,
　　　　　　　　　　The Plane of the Jars,
　　　　　　　　　　　　Is bombed by the U.S.
　　　　　　　　　　In the Secret War
　　　　　　　　　　　　Hands up to stop the
　　　　　　　　　　　　　　fighting,
Garrett and Keo visiting the The half melted Buddhas
　　In The Sim,
　　　　In Vientiane's harmony and peace
Waiting for the winds
　　At the fire-domed temples of the kingdom's heat,
　　　　Salt and light,
　　　　　　In The Golden Triangle of mysteries.

MORAL CRISES

I dream as I lie at the edge of the city
   Of the hub...
      Pulse of deep familial love.
Lost children taken from immigrant families
   By executive order,
      Children imprisoned at the Southern border,
The secrets of souls blocked by fear,
   Silenced by the trauma of tears.
Who is safe in the blue flames
   Smelling of gunpowder and wounds?
We ache as the rubble of centuries
   Returns to us in genocide's wind
      Echoing "Never Again," "Never Again."

ENTERING THE DIVINE THROUGH THE ABSURD

"Long life,

Honey in the heart."

-Mayan expression

For Hugh and Jeanne Joudry

Entering the divine
　Through the absurd
　　The fractal spiral of the polar vortex,
　　　Outsider artists painting the mountain's soul,
　　　The infinite strangeness
　　　In the sulfurs of love
Entering into the blue flames of destiny
　Climbing the mountain
　　With Egyptian tears in vials for kings
Dreaming the jade tablets,
　The sacred green trees,
　The mountain's winds,
As crows watch over our humanity
　Opening to the mysteries,
　　Blessing us with scarlet light,
　　　As honey burns.

ENTERING THE DIVINE THROUGH THE ABSURD 2

The Bael-Shem Tov told stories
  In the town of the
    Hidden mystics
      The Tzaddic's healing wisdom
        Inspiring Jews to rise up
          From the roots of their souls.
Divine Providence
  Revealing the beauty of song
    The Neshuma of the bees mystery
      Mother-tongue circling
        This season of forgiveness,
          Incantations vanished
            In high winds,
Sounding the shofar
  From the red tents of fear,
    Entering the divine through the absurd,
      Do you hear?

DARK IN RADIANCE

Listening to Shekinah's song
  At the burned synagogue near the Dead Sea
    Unwrapping the burned scrolls
      In the House of Rain
Guided by voices of Bukharian Jews
  Teaching us the secrets of Tikkun,
    "To heal and repair the world,"
      Sun rising over the earth
        Gathering us
At the Tree of Life Synagogue
  Grieving today
    For those killed by Hate,
      Jews aiding refugees
        Condemned to death
          For Believing...
            May your souls
              Dark in Radiance...
                Rest in Peace.

THE ARCHEOLOGY OF SOULS

For Fred, who died on Passover, 2008

Mountains surround us.
    The charred solitude of lapis and pine
        Burns within.
            Your "ghost archeology" of souls
                Hidden in my veins
                    Of hand blown glass
                        Enters the cemetery with me.
We picnic with crows
    Eating matzah for the days to come
        "Bread of faith"
          "Bread of healing"
            "Bread of bees"
            "Bread of love."
Listening to Flory Jagoda sing
    "Pesach ala mano"
    "Passover is with us."
Friends blue moon crescendos
    Take me through the turquoise smoke
        Of the jade tablets
           To the mountain's mystery of hope,
              Lapis slate
                Passed rubies in the mud
                  The winds ancient scree
                    Wrapped in a shroud of love.

PRECIPICE

Jumping off,
  He broke from his family,
    Broke the ancient fear
      Beginning in himself
Broke the silence,
  Shattered the morning,
   Splintered the bone
There will be no rising,
  Hear the wind blow,
    There will be no rising,
     Hear the wind blow
Wash away the moment's
  Ancient cry
    Of the man-child
     Pacing to affirm/deny
      At the edge of the precipice
     Hear the wind blow.

AZURE

For HJ

When you were a garbage man
  On Buffalo's West Side,
    Elvis jumped on your truck,

    "Oh don't you step on,
      Step on my Blue Suede Shoes,"

        You accidentally poured ashes
          On his white silk suit,

            Entering the night
              With rhinestones pouring over you.

FUN-HOUSE

In the fun-house at Steeplechase
   Where clowns hit us with sticks
      And hot air machines blew up
         Grandmothers' skirts
            So people in the audience
               Could see their underwear,

We noticed we were on a stage
   Where people paid to see the show,
      "Was this the grotesque,"
         I asked my father?

I was seven years old
   And breathed deep,
      As clowns cracked their whips
         Behind us.

OLD NEIGHBORHOOD

For Marvin and Gail Keifer

Mazy worked the bumper cars
  At Coney Island,
    Madam, at Knickerbocker Village,
      Near the Manhattan Bridge, in New York,
        Inspiring kids to perform outrageous acts
        Of courage,
          Mazy, wearing blatant makeup and scarves.

Walking passed the tenements on Cherry Street,
  One half mile from Gus's pickles
    On Essex Street

The smell of fish-blood from
  The Fulton Fish Market on South Street,
    And your father's death,
      Killed by a knife,
        In the early morning.

EXTRAVAGARIA:
AND PAY MY DEBT TO THE BOATMAN'S DREAM.

"En el tundo del pecho estamos juntos.
In the depths of our hearts we are together."

-Pablo Neruda

EXTRAVAGARIA 1:

And Pay My Debt to the Boatman's Dream

"To the eye of the spiral we fly
From the luminous fires of love, we
return."

-Terry Hauptman

"Violence has changed me."

-Louise Glück

Here where the soul breaks the sea
Aleppo's children exiled in sulphur, scream
I take my place trembling in wild bees
Here where Syrian women in Brooklyn on Avenue B
With long blue painted moons on their fingernails, breathe
Listening to the March of the Imagistas on the street
Praying for those exiled under siege
Lifting the mineral veils of refugees
I take my place trembling in wild bees
And pay my debt to the Boatman's dream.

EXTRAVAGARIA 2:

But the Light Will Give Us No Peace

"But the light will give us no Peace."

-Louise Glück

Survivors distill the cries of the world,
"But light will give us no peace."
Shattered songs disgrace us in tyranny
Abandoning the dark/light radiance for grief
I take my place trembling in wild bees
Here where the soul breaks the sea
Where fragments of fragments, shards of shards scree
Falling into the arms of grief
In the wolf winds of brutality
I take my place trembling in wild bees
And pay my debt to the boatman's dream.

ANCESTRAL

Ferrying our way to Christ Church
Passed Waitomo's glow worm caves
Throwing off sparks from the music of wild bees
And onto Hokateka's sea,

The Maori people welcoming us
To the center of the world
"Te Maunga" What is your mountain?
"Te Moana"   What is your river?
"Te Whare"   What is your home?

Guiding us under the blue blood moon
Passed Rotorua's heartbeat
Listening to Kiri Te Kanawa's *song
Where crows scream,

I remembered my Great Grandma Rae's green eyes
And her fortunetelling gleam,
Supporting herself
With song and dance routines
And paid my debt to the boatman's dream.

*Magnificent Maori Opera Star

RETURN TO LA PAZ:
PEACE BE WITH YOU

For Luis Ramos   (1950-2016)

"I'm hiding in the back of your highest spirit."
-Luis' translation from the Mayan of Jesus' last words.*

I will always remember
    Your heartbeat drum
        And the night we drummed
            As a family on La Salle
                In Harlem.

My mother asking for a faster beat
    And you chanting
        "Follow your heart   your heart."

We wept when you stood
    Under the chuppah
        With my sister
            Your long black Aymara hair
                Down to your waist

My sister Helen's radiant beauty
    Enchanting
        When the moon was turquoise.

You return to La Paz
    The high mountains of Bolivia
        Where you were born

Your sisters, Yola, Juana, Rosa
    Scatter your ashes
        In the Altiplano winds.

73

We weep over your early death
　　Ache for your health
　　　　Lost long ago
　　　　　　When you were named Vicente
　　　　　　　And you painted Tupac Katari,
　　　　　　　　The eighteen century revolutionary
　　　　　　　　　Fighting for social justice
　　　　　　　　　Flayed in the plaza

Wearing your miner's cap
　　Fighting for the Bolivian people
　　　　The Zaponistas singing your name.

We weep for your spirit of the condor
　　And the promise to Helen, my sister
　　　　That was broken long ago,

*The Mayans believe the last words Jesus said were, in Mayan: "Eki-Lamah-Sabatani." These words were immediately translated into Spanish: "Me escondo trasel pieroma de tu ses." "I'm hiding in the back of your highest spirit." Told to me by Luis Ramos.

EL ILLUMINADO

(d. 1596)

For Gerald McBride

Luis de Carabajal
Arrested by la Inquisición
Tortured at the stake in Mexico City,
Heretic Judaizer
Conjuring sacred memory
As The Song of Songs
Burns in cantillating rain
Lightning and winds
Calling to the disappeared
Condemned to silence.

      El Illuminado,
      How deep your hunger
      As your spirit shakes the soul
      As night falls
      Dreaming Sefirah of
      High desert sanctuarios
      Gathering the sparks
      On the wheel of light,
      Your scorched parchments
      Concealing the mysterious
        Vision of be shem Adonoi
        Tzevaot*

*In the name of the Lord of Hosts.

DREAMSONG

For Gerald McBride

Wandering with you on Canyon Road in Santa Fe's
   Ancestral winds,
Singing corridos, as history unfolds before you,
As angels turn to meet you for a coffee
   At La Fonda,
With your Great Grandfather,
   At the House of the Blues.
Following you passed La Casa Sena
   Listening to María Dolores Pradera sing
      "Habaneras de Seville"

Wandering with you in dreams
   Passed The El Rey Theater
      In downtown Albuquerque

And then, passed your Great Grandfather's (x7)
   Adobe hacienda
      In Abiquiu

Through Georgia O'Keefe's black door
   Following blackbirds in the Bosque
      Through your quetzal flame
         The plumed serpent of friendship's song

Painting Georgia's Ghost Ranch cry
   In duende's nightwinds,
      Under the ex-voto sky.

BREAD OF LOVE

For Gerald McBride

Rune of the dark tree's incendiary breath
Bending deep in the earth's ash
Where sap runs blood
In the raven-wind,
River of the dead
Crouched at the roots
   Of friendship
      And the zig-zag lightening
      of the sacred Berdache*

Zohar in the hollow of trees
The silver teeth of hidden alphabets
In the Russian olives and piñon pines,
The amber soot of memory,
Zig-zags over the windwalking land

    Duende's gash of iridescence
      In the agony of doves
      As night breaks open
      Like a love song.

*Spirit/seer of man and woman.

MAESTRAPEACE

The Women's Building,
San Francisco

for Annice Jacoby

Beautiful again
  The sea-sulfur radiance
    Of women
      Walking with lilies.
Yemayah rising up out of the painted waves
  The Aztec goddess Coyolxauhqui
    Teaching Peace
      From the center of the world.
Rigoberta Menchu
  Shining visionary light
    From her visionary life
      As night shines her
        Burnt lilac lunar ash
          Hyacinth fire
            Magnificence
              Her Maestrapeace
                Into the winds
                  Of Mayan prayer.

EX-VOTO

For Annice Jacoby

"The duende then, is a power, not a work, it is a struggle,
not a thought. I have heard an old maestro
of the guitar say,"The duende is not in the
throat, the duende climbs up inside you, meaning
this: it is not a question of ability, not of
true living, style, blood, of the most
ancient culture of spontaneous creation."

-Federico García Lorca

Flinging gold leaf and pomegranate seeds,
Like rubies in the mud,
Carrying your Frida Kahlo pizza box
Through the Mission District,
And at La Galería de la Raza
Wearing your hummingbird-thorn necklace
Walking between angels taking selfies
Singing Ave Maria
With The Virgen de Guadalupe following you
Passed the ginkgo ovaries of trees,
The lilacs grenadine flames,
Watching the world break open
Like a love song.

EL DÍA DE LOS MUERTOS

The Day Of The Dead
Ex-Votos 2

We crush marigolds under
  The bitter melon moon,
    The blood-jade chrysalis
      Hangs upside down,
        Secreting silk threads
          From the secret place
            Through which the caterpillar is born.
Black butterflies on the keyboard,
  Play the blues.
    My mother hums
      Arranging the furniture in the Bronx,
        Believing all will be new
          In the storytelling twilight,
            As dreamtime eggs
              Break open on
                La lumina de sueños firescapes,
                  Ex-votos singed in the light.
                    Whose taffeta dress
                      And horsehair crinolines
                        Hang between the veils?
You never knew my imperfections
  Were my gifts
    Making the invisible/visible
      This Day of the Dead.
        Who turns you around
          On Milagros' windy street
            Listening to snails singing?

IN THE POMEGRANATE ASH OF BEGINNINGS

Los Alamos, New Mexico

"The phosphorescent glow of decay."
-Meridel LeSueur

For Joel Weishaus

In the pomegranate ash of beginnings
   Blackbirds seed dissonance
      Circling the earth
         Heartbone cracked
            Plutonium of steel guitars
               Rotting in desert heat
                  Of Indian Boarding Schools.

If we forget our grief
   In Los Alamos winds,
      Babies dead from the yellow powder
         Spread to Enewetak Atoll*

In the manganese sulfur
   Of Cante Jondo's
      Atomic scream
         Splashed with silver
            Where Las Vegas New Mexico conversos
               Ride shadow horses
                  Into the next world
                     Writing on Fire
                        Writing on wind

The Pajarito Plateau
   And the piñon pines
      Shattered forever

While children eat ash
In the dark-light
Of burnished stars.

*43 nuclear tests were fired at Enewetak, an atoll in the Marshall Islands, after the Second World War. Residents were evacuated. As told to me by Joel Weishaus.

LUMINOUS SOUL

For Emma Miles

Ask for the impossible
    Singing rapture's dark winds,
        Your heartbeat mystery
            Pulsing in bloodroot,
                Listening to the music of trees,
                    The voice of the voiceless,
                        Daring to breathe free.

Ask for the impossible
    Resettling refugees
        Where the green ants dream,
            Dark in resonance,
                Praising Coltrane's
                    "A Love Supreme."

The blue palms of promise
    From your soul house
        Shapeshifting the ether's fray,
            Today and every day
                Coming back to yourself
                    In hyacinth fire
                        Seeding stars,

Madonna of the crescent moon,
    Branching the twilight
        In the nights and days
            As lavender veins crimson
                We sing your praise.

PARKLAND STUDENTS AT THE CENTER OF THE WORLD

Alyssa Alhadeff, Scott Bergel, Martin Duque Anguiano, Nicholas Dworet, Aaron Feis, Jaime Guttenberg, Chris Hixon, Luke Hoyer, Cara Loughran, Gina Montalto, Joaquin Oliver, Alaina Petty, Meadow Pollack, Helena Ramsey, Alex Schacter, Carmen Schentrup, Peter Wang*

> *"No se ecucha nada más que el llanto*
> *Nothing else is heard but the*
> *weeping"*
> -Federico García Lorca

Parkland students break open the silence
    On gun control
        Break open the firebud of the future
            Demanding no assault weapons
            Thorough background checks

Pushing us forward to forever's pulse
    In the face of danger
        In the face of hope
            After deep loss, terror and pain,
                "And nothing else is heard but the weeping."
"Never Again," will children be lost to gun violence,
    Lost to the NRA's rule.
Anhinga's screamed at the death of students gunned down
    Near the slash palm and the saw palmetto,
        Deep cries in the lilacs' smoke wrapped dawn,
        Parkland students leading us all
            In the change to come.

*The names of the dead victims from the Stoneman Douglas High School shooting, Feb 14, 2018.

DEFORESTATION

The Amazon forest burns through
   The horned moon's
     Mouth of fear
The blood-red heat of molten earth
   Flames in agony
     Moans like jackals
       Flanked by bees
In the smoke of sinewy animal hearts
   Fanged by petrified hope
     Trembling in prayer

PANDEMIC:
THE FIRE IN THE GODS' EYES

"The terrible grief of being human."

Rumi

Dead bees inside God's fire
  As we cherish the night,
    Keeping hope alive,
      Cherish the night's green winds
        Between the shadows
          Before they shatter exiled song,
        The world's grief
         A pandemic of fear.

Light a candle for ancestral prayers,
  The lost dreams and mysteries
    Never to be shared
      Singing deep songs for
        The dead and the living
          As terror flails
            And the winds break open.

AFTERWORD

I first met Terry Hauptman when she was a graduate student here in Albuquerque, and we became fast friends. I was immediately impressed with her love of world literature and especially poetry, her passion for art and world music, and her extraordinarily kind and generous spirit. She was always encouraging and accepting, inclusive and eclectic, a true and honest friend, and a poet's poet. Her passion for writing and painting has never subsided, and her literary and artistic output is, in a word, phenomenal.

As I read her latest book of poems, Rubies in the Mud, I am enchanted once again by her unique mastery of musical language, her vivid and sometimes unexpected imagery, and the love and warmth that pervades all of her work. Her poetic juxtapositions are always profound and sometimes evoke a surreal quality that is altogether marvelous. Rubies in the Mud is divided into sections, each with its own theme, and I noticed her many tributes to and fascinating memories of her sisters, her parents, her grand-parents, and great-grand parents, her aunts and uncles, her daughter and husband, her intriguing and proudly radical relatives, and her vast network of close and inspiring friends. They are all fodder for her incredible poems, as are the great heroic figures of history that she also honors.

I feel like I am part of Terry's world when she remembers her mother "humming at Empanadas Cafe", or as "new mothers cry their green willow prayers wearing destiny's necklace of stone tears as the sky turns red." In "Beloved of the Soul 2" we are witness to " the comings and goings of angels in tablets lost in storms." In the delightful "Post Card" we meet "Great Grandma Rae" reading fortunes at Coney Island. In "You Follow the Stars", we see "Grandpa Charlie" and his "wild dance at Bickford's" and "How we would dance for you, dance for your socialist dreams."

In "Ex-Voto" we think of "Flinging gold leaf and pomegranate seeds, like rubies in the mud, carrying your Frida Kahlo pizza box, through the mission district, and at La Galeria de la Raza wearing your hummingbird-thorn necklace walking between the angels taking selfies... the lilacs grenadine flames, watching the world break open like a love song." We get to share Terry's love for the beauty, sounds, sights, smells, and rhythms of Jewish, Latino, Indigenous, African, and all the many cultures that she has encountered and paid homage to in her poems.

My hat is off once again to the magnificent Terry Hauptman and her wonderful new book, Rubies in the Mud. The book's poems are to be read over again, even aloud, and savored with each reading.

-Poet Gerald McBride
Albuquerque, New Mexico

BIOGRAPHY

Rubies in the Mud is Terry Hauptman's sixth volume of poetry. She is the author of five previous full length poetry collections: *Masquerading In Clover: Fantasy of the Leafy Fool,* with hand-painted plates (Boston: Four Zoas, 1980), *Rattle* (Tulsa: Cardinal Press, 1982), *On Hearing Thunder* (St Cloud, Minnesota: North Star Press, 2004), *The Indwelling of Dissonance,* (St Cloud, Minnesota: North Star Press, 2016,) and her most recent book of poems, *The Tremulous Seasons,* (St Cloud Minnesota: North Star Press, 2019.) She holds a Master's Degree in Poetry from The University of New Mexico, Albuquerque, where she studied with our poet laureate, Joy Harjo, and a Ph.D in Interdisciplinary Arts from Ohio University. She reads her poetry rhapsodically and exhibits her luminous 5'x40' Songline Scrolls nationally. She has taught World Art, Poetry, and Ethnopoetics at several universities and workshops, most recently at Green Mountain College. She lives in Vermont with Robert and Kira.